WOMEN

of

AMERICA

WOMEN

of

AMERICA

POEMS

CHARLIE SMITH

W. W. NORTON & COMPANY

NEW YORK / LONDON

The characters, descriptions, and events depicted in these poems
do not connote or pretend to convey private information
about anyone living or dead.

For information about permission to reproduce selections from this book,
write to Permissions, W. W. Norton & Company, Inc.,
500 Fifth Avenue, New York, NY 10110.

Manufacturing by The Courier Companies, Inc.
Book design by JAM Design
Production manager: Andrew Marasia

Library of Congress Cataloging-in-Publication Data
Smith, Charlie, 1947–
Women of America : poems / by Charlie Smith. — 1st ed.
p. cm.
ISBN: 978-0-393-32735-9
1. Love poetry, American. 2. Women — United States — Poetry. I. Title.

PS3569.M5163W66 2004
811'.54 — dc21

2003013971

W. W. Norton & Company, Inc., 500 Fifth Avenue, New York, N.Y. 10110
www.wwnorton.com

W. W. Norton & Company Ltd., Castle House, 75/76 Wells Street, London W1T 3QT

1 2 3 4 5 6 7 8 9 0

CONTENTS

Eastern Forests   13

There's Trouble Everywhere   14

What This Stands For   16

Women of America   18

Monkeys in White Satin   20

On Not Buying a Cellphone   21

Recall   23

In July   24

Shame   25

My Wild Nights   26

After Haydn   28

Compared to What   30

In Bahia Honda   35

Modern Art   37

"Dem Bones"   38

I Mean Everything I Say   40

Late Days   41

Pursued by Love's Demons   45

Solitude   46

Old Business   47

Landscapes   48

Talking to Whom   53

Each Night I Enter a Terrible Silence   54

Refuge   55

Call Girls   56

The Night Won't Stop It   58

Creation Rites   59

Someone Still Capable of Change   60

A Selection Process   61

Excursion   62

Portents   63

The Light Shining Now   64

Still the Moment Intends to Replace Us   65

Religious Art   66

Arrangements   67

Magnificat   68

Indications   69

Ceremonies   70

Passing Through   71

Sprung   72

Material Essential to the Production   74

True Art   75

Towns Along the River   76

Dusk at Homer's   77

Day 7/24   79

Common Knowledge   80

Rain West of Marfa   82

New Jersey Transit   87

The Moment Preceding   88

Little Paradise   89

Old Nobodies Traveling Alone   90

The Wilderness   92

Dusk, Like the Messiah   95

To Daniela

ACKNOWLEDGMENTS

Barrow Street: "Material Essential to the Production," "Towns Along the River"
Chelsea: "Excursion"
Five Points: "Compared to What," "In July," "Landscapes," "My Wild Nights,"
    "Old Business"
Hanging Loose: "Late Days"
The Kenyon Review: "Day 7/24," "I Mean Everything I Say"
The Nation: "Pursued by Love's Demons"
The New Republic: "The Moment Preceding"
Open City: "A Selection Process"
The Paris Review: "Recall," "Women of America"
Poetry: "After Hadyn," "Arrangements," "Eastern Forests," "In Bahia Honda," "The Light
    Shining Now," "Modern Art," "New Jersey Transit," "On Not Buying a Cellphone,"
    "Portents," "Refuge," "Sprung," "Still the Moment Intends to Replace Us," "There's
    Trouble Everywhere," "What This Stands For"
Rattapallax: "Little Paradise," "Talking to Whom"
Solo: "'Dem Bones'"
Southern Review: "Call Girls," "Monkeys in White Satin," "Shame"
Southwest Review: "Dusk at Homer's"
Tin House: "Solitude," "The Wilderness"
The Virginia Quarterly Review: "Ceremonies," "Creation Rites," "The Night Won't Stop
    It," "Someone Still Capable of Change"

Poetry After 9/11: An Anthology of New York Poets: "Religious Art"
The Best American Poetry 2003: "There's Trouble Everywhere"

I would like to thank the John Simon Guggenheim Foundation and the National
Endowment for the Arts for fellowships that helped during the writing of this book.

WOMEN

of

AMERICA

EASTERN FORESTS

I have been walking in the eastern forests
through everglades and hammocks into a mixed deciduous woodland
where hummingbirds and woodpeckers cohabit in the downy hawthorn bushes
and the pepper-and-salt skipper moth, hunted
by the white-eyed vireo and other creatures,
batters its way through broken branches of shortleaf pine
and smooth sumac, a senseless bug without what we call heart,
though as everyone knows some intention, impervious to special pleading,
propels this creature and the eastern black oak acorn weevil,
among thousands of others, across vast reaches of transition, mixed
deciduous and oak-hickory forests, along with wood frogs and flying squirrels,
like love does in our nomenclature, or rumors of gold.

THERE'S TROUBLE EVERYWHERE

There the blind man and his personal dark,
dawn like an emission between buildings,
arrested in the street a second,
meline, no, saffron, a peckish, dilute yellow
and uncontrollable like the light in
a Lorrain painting,
the dawn bearing down out
of its momentary stall,
there the blind man avec dog,
a man who can't suddenly dash
across the street crying *Martha, is it you?*
but must wait
for the dog's slow mind to consider
the next step. And those black wings leaving the scene,
the creases of analgetic green in the young trees
like the heaviness in the shoulders
after adolescence, the
description of life's deeper meaning
in the curve of the homeless man's body, asleep
on his sweater, the young woman walking fast
who looks as if small bits of veneer
have been chipped away, these
speak of something important just arriving.
An old obsession's slowly dying. The day
refers to itself in the third person, like the grinning maniac
who greets you as if he knows you. It's always
morning somewhere, you think,
but this doesn't have any hold on you now.
Even as you move you are reaching back
for something, some lien on existence
you remember, some slab or kitchen step you sat on
listening to the interior noises, the rhythm — you

say to yourself now—of a continuity
you haven't been able to find since,
but it isn't that easy, and it never was.
Always some criminal loose on the property,
moving closer. Some name you
once went by
inscribed inside the wedding band
of an unidentified corpse pulled from the river.
And the love you were so sure of,
that appears like a shape in the trees
on a leeward reach, the vast greenery
uprooted from some rain forest empire,
squeaks and trembles, or this
is only the blur cornering on Tenth.
Whatever might change what's wrong
won't declare itself. And the young poet,
an austere woman briskly climbing
the stairs at the Cineplex, looks
haggard and close to despair,
but says nothing as you pass; it's not necessary
at this time to beg rescue, not yet,
though summer's heavy on the town,
and the well-watered lawn
by the cathedral's not open to our citizens.

WHAT THIS STANDS FOR

Plum bushes unable to bear
    the light and the pond that has no place to hide
the reeds saying save me save me are lying

as are the deer imitating lawn ornaments
    and the cherry trees with their little pink
collapsable mouths. The greasy surf,

triplicated and distressed,
    mixed in design, performs
its one trick, lying about it, too,

promoting its complexity,
    which is nothing of the sort. The stupid desire
to find something else with an interior light, some bug

or monkey,
    some planet or lover turning away,
the sexual context of memory

is almost too much
    in this beachy spring with its wet towels
and donuts

gritty with aspirin dust,
    the rabbits like small brown hats
littering the yard.

Here comes that feeling again,
    the emotional ineptitude that abruptly picks up its bed
and walks, that you come on later standing drinks

   . . .

and roaring, the one that knows
        how to deal with difficult women
and the dark innuendo everyone calls a love life.

WOMEN OF AMERICA

On the pale morning I left town
I was thinking about women,
and later, in the Rockies where work was scarce,
I thought of women all day
and pretended I was in Florida, for example,
at the little business opportunity my friend Calico
ran in the mall at Perry. By roads in the desert
and among the bean fields in California
I thought of women and
preserved this huge interior life for them
like an estate sheltered from creditors.
It was better, like Dante, to have the woman
out of sight, to spend my time thinking about her,
like Petrarch, like the crippled Leopardi, Keats
and all the rest, to save myself the trouble of real life
and the provincialisms of fact, all that,
the women somewhere maybe in heaven
or upstate New York, doing something
besides thinking of me, I didn't mind,
the conversation went on anyway, its riches sustained me,
the complex multifactors crossing
and intermixing like a high school band
in its difficult formations. Everything else
was simple gesturing, an arm reaching out a car window
to hand someone a sandwich. Of what this came to,
I can't really speak, the women
in their trials and compacts, their anguished disputes
outside small-town jails, of these
I have nothing to say. I was seized by thought,
on a pale morning in Alabama,
distracted as I pumped gasoline, wondering

about Hazel and the grip
she still had on me—How so, Hazel, I thought,
and thus time began to pass, in America.

MONKEYS IN WHITE SATIN

Now and then you catch a glimpse of space invaders
moving around under the bridge — campers, someone says.
Once — this may be a dream — the road by my house
was lined with blossoming plums. White like
the foamy sweat of torture victims,
residue of tessellated stars, something less particular
than we would have liked. Convinced of my importance
I moved to another town. No one even noticed
how benumbed I was. You could get a monkey
back then for a pet. Always, without exception,
you'd regret it if you did. Later we were at the beach,
old friends, or calling ourselves such,
the tide a dark hesitating force that came on anyway,
like some reference you made to what's next in line
that you said meant nothing, wasn't your intention at all.

ON NOT BUYING A CELLPHONE

Late snow a re-snow,
callback, comeback, return by way
of a vanishing point,
blossoms in the pear tree re-doubled,
amplified, spring recused,
on hold, conferenced out
as I enter the cellphone store.
I'm wondering if I buy a phone
will there be a new set of people to call.
For sixty dollars
you can have the whole country.
By contract
crouch in the dark hall
calling for a consultation with California.
The snow—that doesn't pick up—
is falling as we speak. It's April,
that ugly little month, so characterless
and snappy, such a ukelele playing
inutile month, wallet stuffed
with IDs, a sap. And snow
and cellular distractions
meaningless against the large psychological
questions. What
of a tendency toward bombast,
and the vast promisings
and the late-night ineffectualisms,
the sordid vague confessions
in person denied? What to address,
what coordinates give in the health-food store
among the whispery silky milks,
the pressings
from peas and pears and

squeezings of grape and obscure
Ethiopian legumes,
the earth wringings
sweat of melon and leakage
from the side of China? Still
it's snowing, still the tremor
and the crashing in the heart, and what to say.

RECALL

Old cadences, cracklings along the sight line,
your arms thrown back, I remember this,

the tortured way with your second language,
what was instrumental, the spiritual phrasing,

cups of tea, an afternoon in Venice
overcoming resistance, who could forget,

you said: *The garden like a strangled lover*
lies heaped upon itself,

and no one laughed, the stillness of the afternoon,
electrical cicadas, the sun offering

to pay for everything, the world filled
to the brim, you noticed this, later the star

jasmine vines stripped naked,
hurricane disorderly and evil-tempered,

like us, you said, everything just then—painted plates,
the operatics—referring to this.

IN JULY

In July when meat smoke
fills the town,
that's when I think
of you. And June, too,
I thought of you in June.
And in the months before that.
A string of time's divisions, all
of them inky
with little dots where I
thought of you.
Certain places soaked
with you, like the towels they used to
mop up the lemonade.
I thought of you
in the band concert
when the tubas
sank down into their difficult valley.
And later at the reception
where a boy dropped a slice of yellow cake
into the punch.
In July the barbecues begin.
As if it's then the cows reach the market,
meat available.
In China, they say,
men fish with nets in the little streams.
Landlords watch them, waiting
for their money.
If I was there,
an intense person, watching his net
settle onto the current,
I'd think of you, that's obvious.

SHAME

I keep referring to you in transition from
one state of being to another like a woman you see
on two or three different buses in the same afternoon.
But this is not shame exactly or anything numinous
and I can't tell you how badly
I want to get high and walk under big complicated trees
and keep talking about you
until you show up. Love goes like this: You forget.
I'm trying not to let this happen, it's a kind of workout
I'm giving myself, high impact, me pounding against
your silence. They all know where you are.
And foolishly I haunt the stockyards and the record stores.

MY WILD NIGHTS

What I took to be spirit
was only the small pick work
plastered over by flesh,
skin tags
and goitrous protrusions,
some way of putting things
designed to make you believe
I was one of the elect
one who knew what it was like to stick
with his suffering long enough
for the suffering to ignite
clarification
of the mysterious ways of God
to man. My wild nights
of speculation
bore this hollow fruit.
Every lie I told
each made-up scrap
was part of this. (Yet the spirit
slipped in.) Where
might what I looked for be? —
I couldn't get this out of my mind.
I humiliated myself, and
sometimes others,
and couldn't stop
for the body count.
I never could quit lying.
And my loud protests
the singular phrasing
I memorized from a book,
these were particularly galling.
I stopped asking questions.

I *took* questions
gave answers that
grated the flesh off the inside
of my mouth. Each place I looked
the spirit
lay in wait like
an animal sent to fetch me.
Even that walk
on the ruined street
those boys
couldn't say enough about,
and your hand on my arm,
I didn't realize this, too,
was a spiritual thing.
I couldn't say what I meant.
I offered an obviously
miscreantic praise.
Later became a man
of whom they asked—
A friend of yours?

after Amiri Baraka

AFTER HAYDN

Speeding around in a little car
driving over things, you keep alert
for changes
too circumstantial & exact
to be noticed. Crepy sky
over Manhattan. In your head
the same four-beat Rexrothian line
as last night beats on. Someone's grandfather
killed by a drunken driver and you make yourself
think what this means: drunken: alien,
so magical, an irrepressible
       voodoo snatching the loved one away.
Otherwise you're obsessed
with the past, a fantasy junkie.
The stoop,
painted pink this week
by the grieving super,
iridescent really,
like Cuban architecture—
this begins to operate on you,
saves you, you might say—rescue by distraction—
and you press on with a new thought,
notice the sky: corrugated, fish-scaled,
the clouds choppy & layered. You're an
adventurer, that's the word: Paris,
the irregular watering stops of Upper Egypt,
truck towns and villes
like rural hamlets
       down south: no new stores
but for the video place, a barbecue shack.
Prayer, family, a certain
set of the jaw, in a spot like that,

tie things together. What's the line? The Rexroth?
It's—*something*—the bindery—*something:*
all things tied together
in some way, a symphonist's idea,
I wonder how often real life comes up with it,
maybe just a dream.

COMPARED TO WHAT

The way certain rogues get to us,
the way, coming into a town,
the tottery chimneys, the creamery,
the boy stumbling as if he understands what it is to be broken,
the way these move us slightly.

* * *

And how on another day
someone takes a room in a hotel and calls a few friends,
and orders a prostitute,
and tells her a story
of paddling a boat among drifting flower gardens,
and the woman, who is not interested, who is thinking of soup
or an envelope waiting at home,
shifts toward the man
lightly touching him, grazing his arm,
without feeling anything for him,
simply doing what she is paid to do, and the man,
who knows this, and doesn't care especially,
is thinking of the flowers drifting in the river, gardenias and roses,
and of a gar, silvery and sharp like a sword, cutting just under the surface.

The way when we hear this we sink down
as if we are entering a small enclosure in our minds
and are suddenly overcome with despair.

And there is another story one remembers
in which a young person
comes into money and becomes prideful

and loses everything and takes a job in a sale barn
wearing a straw hat and making jokes that aren't funny,
and as we listen, a sudden, irrepressible tenderness enters us.

Later there will be stories told in basement rooms,
cold sandwiches on a counter
and a faint chilled laughter from the porch,
and someone who hasn't spoken for a week gets up
and pisses noisily in a can . . .

I was thinking of a woman I loved,
who wouldn't love me.
I thought I would never get past this,
and though it was obvious I would,
that we all do, I began to love the pain
that didn't want to go away, and held on to it.

It touches me how ignorant we are
of many simple effects, the way after my
father stamped through the garden his shoes smelled of flowers.
The way as he badgered us we could smell the wet dirt
and the rotted lilies.

And how later we put our experiences to ourselves
with a certain fastidious pride,
and compel ourselves,
as if we are friends of the court,
to address certain facts that would go otherwise unnoticed,
and how there is a way of explaining these conflictions
to a friend
that makes them seen unimportant.

. . .

And the way someone we pass in the street,
an old woman out early
who is too heavy and aches with gout
and favors one grandchild over another and
is slightly desperate and afraid for money—the way
we pass her without caring who she is, and how this
is what it is to be human, no one very close
after all, and how obvious it is—like spring
taking over everything—what we want.

                              *   *   *

Soon it is night again and we are wandering around
outside the house thinking things over,
weighing the dark
like a puppy in our hands,
dividing our life into phases,
trying to place one bit of sadness on top of another,
attempting, so we believe, to experience the whole of ourselves,
which has doubled back,
trying to establish representation
with what is already gone,
sure now there was
nothing we could do to save ourselves
and trying not to be scared by this, comparing ourselves
to someone gentled by loss, to a young teacher perhaps,
standing in a darkening classroom
the day of the hurricane, lingering after the children have gone
watching the sky darken and the wind begin to pick at the trees,
a woman who knows something irreplaceable
is dying in her . . .

        *   *   *

understanding how it is possible to place our whole life
succinctly into a frame such as this,
again and again, yet never able
to turn away and leave it there . . .

trying to make something
up that is strong enough to hold us
or move us or keep us.
Like a man in a field walking in the wind
who briefly forgets himself in the smell of lemon grass,
who comes on a red scurry of fur and bone
and stops, convinced an age of unhappiness has arrived.

                              * * *

Won't you at least, she says, consider
another way of putting things —

and later,
after a good meal, the way we explain we were off our stride,
that is to say impossible to live with . . .

and in the dream, her fiancé's laughter
humiliated us,
the way she wouldn't say where they were going on the honeymoon . . .
for a moment this wasn't a dream . . .

* * *

In Miami the stacked blue waves tumble in.

You can look up a description of the place
in a book in the lobby and and then glance up
and see the "coconut palms
and sparkling pool, the Kontiki bar
and wide white sand beach . . ."

Whatever looks straight, she said,
it might look straight, but it eventually curves.
And I said
is that supposed to mean something?
But by then it was too late to come to an understanding.

* * *

The way occasionally we greet the dawn as if we are responsible for it.

IN BAHIA HONDA

Light a blunder, a gaff,
some lost chance rustling behind a curtain,
a fluttering along the skin of our arms as we sink
into the the feathery limitations of the reef,
bodies cast upon the surface. A grim dust of certitude
covers all, importunate,
a frailty in the transfixed mollusks,
the wan members of cretaceous dynasties
giving up the throne. There's movement
off to the left, fish like tiny gold bugs
hovering in the Brachipoda,
a surge bringing all
to shore like a chronic nausea,
victims in houses
sliding downhill, who know nothing
and go on not looking at you
when you try to help. Do they swim away finally,
at the last moment? The ocean's dirty
and smells of itself,
unwashed, it's been up all night
sitting on a bench in the bus station, crying for its girlfriend.
But no one wants to hear this—who cares—
it's a weekday and we're off work,
Cubanos going in as a family, backed by a radio orchestra.
We've paid $15.50 for equipment, a sack lunch,
and how easy it is for once to drop to our knees.
Here are the adjustments easy to make,
the rescue work we take personally,
goggles going on,
heads slipping under like optiscopes
to view the wary world,

frozen in time,
the flooded area sporting its epicycles and bridgework,
an awful evidence torn to pieces on the floor.

MODERN ART

Matisse, in a letter
to Henry Clifford, said an artist must identify himself
with the rhythms of nature, make effort,
prepare the soil, get down and grub. Where you end up
won't look like the place you started in.
It won't be that place. I'm obsessed with a woman
and each day I invite the shadow shape —
which obsession is — in the door. Lingerer,
vague disamplitude, you're like rain
in the next county. I sense your presence on the breeze,
smell your body in the damp clay and feculence.

[handwritten annotations: "impurities)" and "soil wt impurities)"]

"DEM BONES"

In the country I think of women's hips,
of a particular bowed angularity, the incredible harmoniousness
and universal clarity, the sense of justification in every corpuscle
a woman's body gives me, of the invulnerable breasts, the billowy thighs,
the moist central pavilion—and this is to say nothing
of the extraordinary character of women, the capacity
for sustained amiability, the credulous witticisms and unplanned
extended and moony exchanges, the taunts that shift to sweet
refusals to soft clamors that give way to the sexual mysteries . . .

It's like this in the country where I lie out in the fields at night,
supine in vegetable rows like something dropped from an airlift,
my free hand in a wet oracle, my tongue approaching, my gathered molecules
stiff as a hawk in a fight, hot as a bald spot
under a magnifying glass or a fire in a cotton warehouse . . .
And right over the tops of our bodies (as I'm picturing this)
winds sweep death like tufts of animal fur along the rows,
and once more from long-deserted lives comes forth the opportunity
to be of service, to express a connective garrulousness and
ingenuity that will, for a time, constitute and maintain
affection and a sense of the limitless possibilities of being alive,
love's like this . . .

Out of the wind a woman dives onto my body,
into my country soul, changing my city ways,
dispensing with the gravity of untenable monstrosities
(the misery of being human),
with the confused yet singular choruses of some hymn the "guide" sings . . .
Love is form
and in a world without accidental occurrences, unduplicatible
and unusually investigated (Here's one more trip into the Unknown!)
just to the right of (and not to be confused with) the mistress Donne described

as smelling of pus and rotted cheese, lolling in her arms,
contorted and shuffled by grace (which follows mercy)
we will soon (as if wars were done) draw up our compact,
our truce and promise of mutual surrender, we who have compared
ourselves
to backdoor flagellants and bamboozled senior citizens
poking through the trash behind malls, (increasingly anonymous) love
going tediously on about sunsets and sumptuous Italian genres,
exhibiting a willingness (or tendency) to show
our appreciation for a phrase or a life well put . . .

I know I will succumb soon to the plunderings of time,
to the rifling of my pockets
and memory's slackened muttered reproaches,
I, too, will come on a former self stripping his bride
like a gift of folk art, dreaming even as I caress her
of women, maintaining a complimentary position among tomatoes
and green onions and other truck crops,
yet, even as one who could never be forgiven, I am without confusion
as I approach the pleadings, the promises and simple facts,
like grandparents surprised en flagrante, the wet mouths
like tiny skulls crushed in the hand, unashamed, old lions
who glance up unconcerned from the carcass, going on
through the fall of man, passing this and continuing . . .

I MEAN EVERYTHING I SAY

A boy's first fistfight, he's crying
all the way through it, stupendously alive,
and the girl raging in her room against the elite of the earth,
it's so unconventional, emotion in the chest,
the emptiness after passion, hope like money in a jar,
it's all feeling, expansiveness unwasted & alive, no one
completely understands this, like rain on a clear day,
or amplitude, the unrestricted dispensations,
someone offering a seat, someone hitting wildly back,
the ugly judgment in the plutocrats's eyes,
all from the heart, the jostling
that begins low in the soul, some day in August
when the lover to come, disguised as someone who hates you,
wheels around the corner adjusting her hat,
and that brisk business in the big oaks, wind
conveying some new way of life—or nothing important—
across town, it touches you.

LATE DAYS

1. OUTSIDE LAS VEGAS

In the Silver Dollar john
I place my hand flat on the sink
wrench around
& look at my face to see what happened.
Later I watch someone's neighbor undress
then hit herself across the back with a cat-o'-nine-tails
before lights out. I walk around incognito
in my own home. Dispatcher
of long-distance affections,
the twenty-eighth caller on the call-in show,
the one who gets abruptly nasty & begins to weep,
I signal for a time-out.
My best friend became a doctor at forty,
sits alone
in his office eating sardine sandwiches
practicing his technique.
It's the heart, he says, it's
diabetes, prostate, that'll be two hundred dollars.
We used to strip
down & examine each other's equipment.
Persuaded by the heart of things,
by time spent there alone,
we believed in life, in the life to come.
Now I'm traveling to Mexico by stake truck,
riding in the back. Dressed by a fire,
among friends,
I compare dog bites & episodes w/the Virgin,
and make big claims about my capacity for love.
In the right-
hand pocket of my former life I've left something for you.

That is, darling, your turn will come.
I'd walk out on myself if I could.
I love the distant glow in the nighttime desert sky
like a worn yellow spot in the dark
everything might still slip through.

2. DREAMBOAT

Some starlet grimacing
is my double,
representative of a rankness
since expunged. I go out with producers
& make obnoxious remarks
about friends who've withdrawn all their cash
and some desperate character
turns around in the steak house
with a sneer
& says I know you
better than you know yourself.
It's dangerous down on the piers
where wrath
and meretricious pleading
take the place of God,
but we go there,
summoned by grace,
terrible in our capacity not to love,
we with the roughed-up skin
of old chordate impossibilities,
unexplained to ourselves,
formerly a nuisance
to the neighbors. We can't recall
much of our past except the loveless,
the evil & corrupt
moments we've spent forever
untangling, and go forth,
like rapid response teams
riding in a dream boat,

bunglers, deviates, small-time
swindlers on the romance circuit,
yearning for brevity,
disconsolate
yet stubborn, unappeasable.

PURSUED BY LOVE'S DEMONS

As if the backstreets of our local city
might dispense with their Pyrrhic accumulation of dust and wineful tonality,
offer a reprise of love itself, a careless love
rendered grand and persuasive
by its own shy handful of hope, some ballast such as this
on a summer afternoon when the air smells of slaughtered chickens,
and other problems, like the estranged spouse of a good friend,
holler from the passageway. It's always conclusive
in the bungled moment after you try to accomplish something irreducible.
So you say as you return empty-handed from the store,
having forgotten everything—your money, the list.

SOLITUDE

In the background a disturbance builds:
cammarones; bone spurs;
individualism adding up to what?
You beat about
finding space for all your goods.
I know how it is.
Chunky, ill-defined,
life lumbers on. You wish you could remember
that German word—
      a kind of sugar cake;
the solitude she entered
like a phrase dispelling doubt,
the solitude
entrained and crowded now
something—something—weeded out.

OLD BUSINESS

for L.W.

A quiet joy appears amid loneliness, doesn't
replace it. We pass the South American men
listening to a radio played softly.
We put faith—in love, old songs, grace
like a gold ring
left by the sink—in what abides;
we put faith in what returns, forget
easily. I read a poem;
it's one the poet wrote just before he died.
There's death in the poem, though I don't believe
he anticipated his own. I think he looked up
from the desk a little shaken
and soothed. But even this, someone says,
is no formula, or even an illustration.
The wish to perceive is itself a mistake, limited,
not one of the aspects. Yet we catch sight
of a pattern disappearing in the mix,
waves from a distance
like comb tracks, claw marks,
the young girl in the foreground
lifting her hands into her dark hair.
An amplitude that closes on itself appeals,
a certain wild hillside ransacked by light.

LANDSCAPES

. . . railroad cuts, picked-over scrapyards behind cotton gins,
ornate hibiscus in market gardens
by Sack's Mercantile,
slim, burned-up zinnias behind the barns

red hills lean toward us,
thickets strung with weeds

                              —we got out of the car into Ohio,
failed to conclude things near some blackberry bushes lit
up with tiny white flowers—
                    all brambles, you said,
are beautiful, bushes in a cutover field, too—

certain groves in New England are mysterious and pungent,
avenues of elms rotting in their tracks,
old men loquacious concerning palms, that year in Ponape,
mangroves below Miami like a selection of excuses,
the divided loyalties expressed by sea and sky,
I'm crazy about these,
the way the clouds crouch on the surface of the bay

and there was the time in Wyoming you jumped the fence, rode bareback
over scrubland

            rocks like hailstones, shadows
like trained ponies following, a cave in West Virginia
dipped in salt, fallow patches, tramped on
flattened out earth after the carnival's gone, broken glass in gullies,
ice pools under spruces, the melt and refreeze of these pools,
the way they are clear then turn slowly gray
as if aging, as if decomposing

you noticed the tree thrust in the middle,
these and other evocative areas where the cold collected
that winter we walked in the woods, I think about

and gravel pits, collapsed
grandstands near paved-over cornfields outside Biloxi, Mississippi,
wilderness parks, jungles, embankments
upon which spring makes grandiose, ramshackle statements,

tamarack bogs

there were weeds growing in the eaves of the old house
we slept in the front yard of, wind-snapped pines on a hillside in North Carolina

the way some days end abruptly, you said, like herds
coming out of the bushes
a backing of tropical trees,
all parks, just planted rainy fields, rain in the desert,
lilacs in rain, winter wheat fields in rain,
doves flying in rain over corn stubble,
no, like herds, you said, coming to the river
where there are crocodiles and you can see the grasslands
stretching away blue under the rain,
rained-on beaches,
and freshets and interruptible streams running down to the ocean,
unsorted gray rocks on uninhabited coasts, stubbly with barnacles,
gray days on the lake
a scrap of white cloth you chased
through woods in Maine
cedar billets thickened by rain,
river bends where maples hang like willows over blackwater sloughs
. . .

I think steadily of these

and birches, white-backed and frail, climbing mountainsides,
grain fields, hemlocks near streams, orchards,
all ditches, bleak areas at the edge of cities, areas
of blackened gravel and oily pools draining thickly into swamps
converted into farmland going back to swamp,
drained canals in Illinois, sheared-off hilltops
and hillsides after fire, volcanic slag heaps,
unheroic scuffed patches, addled places and indistinct
shabby gardens without owners or worked-out schemes, cellar holes,
and bosomy hills that were once Indian graveyards,
boys riding backhoes, planting pines, thrusting their fists into the sandy soil,
windy bare mountains I think of,
city dumps pestered by gulls

smooth lawns like huge bearskin rugs,

I love the way the woodland drags its tail to the pond,
seaside swamps, slim conifers covered in road dust, junipers
giving way to myrtle scrub, wild raspberries outside Cape May,
overhangs, arcades
                    trampled weedy places where we lay down

landscapes, you said, that have no appointments to keep

postponed forests, overlooked scarred patches behind factories,
these are fine,
camps in the woods, wet raccoon tracks across tipped granite ledges,
briars at the beach, acres of blueberries, alpine meadows
crossed by deer paths,
                    I go out to stand knee-deep in grass,

in wheat or in ragged oat fields outside Denver,
                              glad I am alive,
someone proposed to and escorted by landscapes, by memories of life
in them, and by the places themselves which never haunt me
but detain me briefly and steadily for conversational
gambits expressed eloquently in memory
or actual declarations composed behind train windows
like pictures moving,
cars spied in a line crossing a bridge in Iowa,
the harsh crying of crows in corn stubble, everything
about our lives together once that charmed me, a memory now

in these places I am happy

by moraines grown up in sorrel, snowfields in intense sunlight,
I give my heart to all weedy lake margins and to ponds thick with bushes,
to ridgelines of several varieties

the confidential remarks of certain summer days
in which we lay on the dried-off slope of a Spanish hill are delightful in memory

I wish I could stand beside you in the Ochlocknee River,
stand in mud, stand in sandy places where the current bells
clearly against the bank, places mussels collect in,
stand in a clear pool and bend my face down to it

there are places in the Okefenokee without material success,
ferny salons behind cypress hammocks,
there are rotting boats at piers now silted in
by streambeds soaked by flood in Minnesota,
vineyards, rutted slopes, forsaken piney woods,
mists like gray fields on the move, precipices, cliffsides,

fragrant areas behind supermarkets,
golf courses, football fields, all grass baseball parks,
fields of crushed brick where buildings used to be

the way certain landscapes, you said, never get anywhere

our old life together grown up in timber,
second and third growth sprung up behind the inextinguishable love
passed now, irreplaceable in memory,
a life I am grateful for

                              explicit, uninterrupted vistas,
rubble fields, salt lakes in the desert,
the rough mountain backs of Nevada,
mines blown open and walked deeply into, canyons
I return to, humbled now slightly, less divided

and canebrakes behind the old house, still standing
years later,

the field still wearing its old clothes,
devil's paintbrush, some yellow bramble
careened into a ditch, the pear trees where
there was once a yard, ragged now, fruit stubbed
off, blackened by time, and
the aged magnolia sporting two huge blooms
like scoops of vanilla spilled on its chest.

TALKING TO WHOM

I am like a man
swallowing small fish whole.
Afterward he watches TV,
coughing quietly into his fist.
If I rub my naked belly around
on the floor, where will you be,
in which room, talking on the phone?
It's at moments like these some tragic
element, some quip
or piece of hotel furniture
flies out the window. Little reaper,
Jefe, there was something else
I wanted to say. I've investigated
all this. And stood among the market's
bright fruit weeping openly.
Dearest, they are tearing
down the movie theaters —
blackened areas in which
we clutched each other,
leaving marks.

EACH NIGHT I ENTER
A TERRIBLE SILENCE

We demonstrated procedures
for each other, taking turns
playing the extraterrestrial. I managed
to corner some affection one night
and gave it to you, a small chunk
you fried up for supper. It took
several glasses to wash it down.
We never could say much
about the future, but insisted on trying.
We thought a lot, but kept it to ourselves.
You were the one passing in the hall
that dark night, a shape like a burglar
I spoke to softly so as not to disturb my wife.

REFUGE

Even as you climb the tenement stairs
you are picturing the disturbances in the dust
behind every door,
the variations of lust and despair
in kitchens too small
to actually cook in. Some dog
barks bitterly and stops. A cry,
some useless interjection, comes
from a blank place in the wall.
Outside the day goes brilliantly
and obliviously on, like a neighborhood genius
who simply won't shut up. Here in the dim
disturbance of your passage—a visitor
showing his new lover
where he once lived—you are already finding
the obscurity you fled. It's still
here and it's no different from what
you keep around the house where you live now.
Only there from the doorway
from which wafts the stinks of rancid blood and
acid burns, does the gleam of
an anonymous eye hint of
another, vaster and more deeply correspondent
crisis, some resolution you have just missed
but should have been here for, that
would have cleared your name.

CALL GIRLS

My rage, you bet,
and its spectacular aftermath, the visits from the cops,
the cut-rate pharmacies where
I bought medicine,
the all-night theaters
I retired to,
let me justify this,
the downtowns deserted by all but their most
persistent citizens,
the cries from two streets
over
as the pack began to circle back,
all this, I promise you,
explicable,
the covenants unalluded to,
the supermarkets I got stranded in,
the old girlfriends I called and out of consideration
for their new circumstances
never identified myself to,
all these,
a matter of reason, of consequence —
the particular block on Sunset
near some palm trees
where I faltered,
unable to go on,
the Mexican couple I mistook for informers,
the spectacular sunsets in that
part of the world,
the slow aging of affection,
the disputes, the roaring in traffic,
the conversion I reneged on,

something—maybe
you remember—to do with pride
and a diffident manner, some idea—
as I said—I was once
devoted to.

THE NIGHT WON'T STOP IT

We are tired of arguing about who is the most hurt.
Better to toddle off for a little Chinese.
The locust flowers each year like cornmeal in the gutters.
An extraordinary way of putting things, saved up
for the love affair of the century,
gets used by a baker's apprentice talking to his dog.
Investors sink back into the shadows.
Someone with a huge capacity for ambivalence nods off.
The cut-rate sky seems for a moment to throb.
Affairs that began in spring's alarming weather die of heatstroke.
A generous gesture hovers in the back of the mind,
but never steps forward. Cravings appear,
like baskets of fresh linen, in the homes of our friends.
Tenderness is appraised and turned in for theft.
The fragrance of dispatched gardens, like a telegram
from the government, is just a memory. It is so fitful,
so desperate, this business of what matters.
Another's down with a stroke. This way of looking at things
will be forgotten. It was only an experiment.

CREATION RITES

. . . some average of the holiness in every person you have run into,
consider this, something like a wall covered in green vines,
an emblem for the spirit, or if not that, what happens when two lovers
stand among bushes in a garden off Houston, arguing a little, but afraid
really to get into it because they fear winding up alone,
and then several music lovers or ex-drug takers wandering along
on a summer day past the restaurant supply stores and the vacant
lot where the wino hotel used to be, they're walking to Chinatown,
these holy people like pilgrims in Benares where they are talking
about putting crocodiles into the river to eat the corpses, you probably heard about it,
and there is some question about procedure in the cremation rites, all that,
but they're obviously part of it, too, the holiness, and still it's summer
and my friend has changed into her bathing suit and is walking
the three blocks to the public pool, it's getting kind of late, she'll swim
twenty laps and finish as the life guard, a slender boy with an island accent,
waits for her to come up out of the water like a rectified god.

SOMEONE STILL CAPABLE OF CHANGE

Aged mothers gape at television.
Father, recently sterilized, putters with his equipment
        in the shed. Quietude, an absence
of spoken plans, the uselessness of revolt, all these

are taught now as electives at the university. Someone
shakes water off his fingers; it looks like light.
        A friend calls to say he's giving up friendship.
A postcard from an ex-lover who wants me to know

she has children now, dozens of them, ha-ha.
And the light dispersing, gusting, crackling as it goes,
        the vast encumbrances of the leaves, the
magisterial roll bars of the big branches,

the strong straight torsos jammed into earth, that night erases.

A SELECTION PROCESS

. . . under unrivaled fresh weather, each day random variations,
assurances come, studious, revised sensibility occupies itself.
I walk around, notice the impeccable configurations,
distortions the breeze replaces itself with
in the large philodendron-like trees, massive
spills of wind, a sort of alternating current
of air streaming above my head. When I am walking
tortured by my disgusting life sometimes
I stop in the middle of an ocean of wind
and begin to make swimming motions or I watch
the patterns the dying sun makes with the big oleanders the
shadows placed artfully against the high school
even doves balanced on an electrical wire can be seen
silhouetted in this arrangement. An old woman carrying groceries
passes on my right, moves her lips slightly but doesn't speak.
Soon, before anyone notices, all this will be gone.
So many claim they lie awake wishing for a new
design, better implants. Yesterday a woman in wind-whipped clothes
led her child on bikes around the corner, admonishing her
to keep pedaling, but the child sped along
I could see in her eyes
her power, the child's power; a distant
line of palms, like fiends in the mind, began to wave.
How close we come, I think, to a life very different from this one.

EXCURSION

The heart moves on, selects a place for itself,
tossed down destitute it rises, only the mind
gives up, a winter's tale
dispersed into scenery around a muddle of ideas,
someone edges out of the park
to say something about irrefutable joy, lost
among the swarming cabs, it rains all afternoon,
streaks on windows, the bays, indented spaces before buildings,
gutters, scuffed patches in Central Park, all fill up,
later we find the subway's a gray lake, a solitary cat swimming,
desolation's investments repay handsomely,
somehow we are not surprised or sidetracked.

PORTENTS

October fades out in its special colors,
wind steps down from the trees,
headed slowly home;
                  the year's a stubborn
pretense now, worn down,
                     worn out.

Meals left in scraps
on the table are cleared away, wine drunk,
the baby sulks and goes to sleep,
and an old woman washes her body carefully,
remembering how they told her to keep it to herself.

Here are smells of baked apples and liniment.
Here are thoughts that gleam a moment, and fade.
Here are the discoveries of age, the resentments,
the papered-over hopes, love a dry tooth in a cup.

One day seeps into the next,
and the next, still dark around the eyes,
looks on without much on its mind.

The nurse beside the bed, who loves baseball,
pats the covers of the dying man,
who smiles, thinking his sister
has come to forgive him, while out at sea
the backs of the waves are spidery white,
and the dark, that has never seen
us in the light, begins to imagine things.

THE LIGHT SHINING NOW

What has begun
atom by atom, the interiority first constructing itself
by ones, a gathering of intent

or simply persistence, the shapes
refined and eventually ejected, this
takes shape like a dawn in gray,

the verifiable aspects of a life
coming together inside the arc of a shell,
the integuments

and masses of centrality, the mollusk body
of love coalescing like birth
in each day renewed,

your various features
and possibilities
placed into their familiar spots,

the light shining now
upon whatever disappeared into dreams,
the nocturnal disbanding

of everything,
particles and selvage
scattered on the floor,

now returned to us, only
a slight recall of the disintegration,
the terror.

STILL THE MOMENT INTENDS TO REPLACE US

The wistful play of dark
descending across the grassy fields,
the shameless way the breeze carries on its
conversation with the carrot weed, the individualized momentum
of each stem and blade
set in motion
across the river where twilight, in compliance
with the statutes, tries again to convince the old houses
it meant nothing by what it said.

There among the debris which seems always to accumulate
around this time of day another
tragedy has taken place, a
loss unexplained but lived through by mice and small rabbits,
the identifiable remains disturbed
so mothers and other close relatives have only memories
that are fading even
as these animals make their way
across the somber and disappearing landscape.

RELIGIOUS ART

Certain precautions, obstacles
set against vandals—the stretch
of highway, for example, outside Nichols, New Mexico,
loneliness like a family art,
a man's idea of himself
pinned down in the Holy Land, strings of peppers
drying on a porch.

I press hard with my feet
against the earth and
call this fighting back. All yesterday
I walked around counting birds.
Trees, a spray of pebbles in the forecourt,
a dip the wind took about six

maintain the posts assigned, repel boarders.

The peculiar emptiness
in the mown hayfield this afternoon
we stood staring into—as a precaution—
the clefts and shadowy declines containing
our deepest interests, the grass shining and then going dull against
the fading light, these were protection enough.

ARRANGEMENTS

I'd like to try a maneuver that doesn't "start in silence
          and end in frenzy," but instead begins
in a terrific caterwauling, thrashing and flailing,
          the fists banging against the floor, cries and
shrieks, appalling in its verisimilitude,
          crashing, writhing delirium, berserk ruction
and development extended into distraught maniacal pleading,
          convulsion, feverish excited speech, hysterical
slapping scenes, a nucleonic furor, and goes
          on from this into an unexpected hallucinatory
passage in which I extoll the beauties of mountain lakes
          at dawn, the strained—while I do this—
look on my face held for hours while I explain
          how beasts and deranged parental figures
did this to me, tried to drown me, all the while
          patting some obviously organic material
I've collected in a sack. You know what
          I'm talking about. Horror at the heart
of beauty. And so I continue, into the whimpering
          and begging stage, the puerile confession episode
in which I convict myself of all manner of hate crimes
          and offer myself up for special punishment.
Then the little chat with the warden.
          A quiet time. Then the priest where I smile sweetly
and enter a beatific state. There's something in my eye.
          I never know who they mean. And despite everything,
silence comes.

MAGNIFICAT

The sky armored behind its rural-style dawn.
I can't tell if it's red, resinous,
minium I mean
or if that's
simply Bonnardesque,
maybe a little puce, puckered
this sunrise
Jan one two thousand—, trimmed
and massive dawn.
The street's lost its passengers,
trees, too,
revealing the silky linings of old coats
hung up there. The overwhelming diversity,
intricacy of life,
its disorderliness,
baffling
to existentialists, is obvious
in every doorway.
For a while
no one's on the street,
but that's not perfection, or even order,
that's a lull. Elsewhere someone's
wrapping a pancake around a sausage, smiling
at a goldfish
in its bowl. Variegations, multi-flecked
and compounded sweetness, joy
like a feather across the lips.
Sometimes nothing
helps, it's so miserable inside and out,
yet still
there's the interjascence
she spoke of, the play
of love's baffling combos, how did we put it?

INDICATIONS

I forgot what I was saving myself for.
And went on setting the table,
giving myself little talks,
observing the natural procession of moments,
you name it, and I said I was saving myself
for great things, but I wasn't.
The woods across the street, the wind
tramping around in the high branches,
the animal life so important to the harmony
of all things—these
gave no real clues as to what was up.
Nothing was up. And the photos we located,
the ones of empty lakes in the North
and old men keeping lookout,
didn't reveal a method.
For years something important,
like a heavy police presence,
waited just around the corner.
The verisimilitude of all things,
the way they seemed almost real,
fascinated me. I thought I was saving myself
for the day when the irresistible showed up,
but this proved to be false. Later
at the Dairy Queen, for a moment
everything fell
into place. Just after this
one of those hummingbirds,
like a red and green bullet that pauses
before it enters your body, appeared,
so excruciatingly beautiful, this kind of death.

CEREMONIES

... way to put it, a seasonal change,
celebration, duck roasting in wine sauce,
the taste of sweet potatoes still in your mouth
when you step out, the afternoon drifting off,
fog on the pond, a New England day in Georgia,
love disputed and continued with, you think
the spiritual life is—what did they say?—
the experience of hashing it out with reality,
that's good, but a somberness in you
nonetheless, a sadness, her soft hand,
the way she knelt with you
to look into her aunt's chest of drawers
at the glass figurines, hundreds of them,
the old woman in another room just dead.

PASSING THROUGH

Strange, the difficulty, or not really, wanting
something so vast, mountains all around, some variation of love's intelligences,
remarkable waters,
a briefly sunlit patch alongside the river,
high bluffs, you reason things out
as best you can,
the dust in small towns
not ancient, old books still unread,
the possibilities not quite endless,
and here as there, homeowners,
two men this time
smile as they go by in their pickup truck,
all indefensible, the green grassy basin
where floods pour through,
every moment is not desperate,
these aged horses
making their way across the field at dusk,
things fit, go onward in the same way
as yesterday, try to,
the girls are growing up again,
wineglasses stacked in a window,
friendship, a long conversation close to dusk,
strange, her voice
recalling another life, as familiar as your own.

SPRUNG

The ministerial shapes of
Chinese women
in the garden I mean, red

fetishistic flowers,
the ropy
sun-damaged hollyhocks

all that's left to put
momentarily against
the crimes of our nature,

the vertigo,
come forth
now, this young boy

among the earnestness
the coziness of commerce,
to carry a hose

and untidily water
everything,
wearing silver bracelets, alone

with his task
as we all are,
the time when dear Kiser

was alive, my parents, too,
and Oscar, and
Kate,

. . .

the boy
missing all those spots,
like I did.

MATERIAL ESSENTIAL TO THE PRODUCTION

. . . lunch money or the coconuts, metastasized wordplay
of the truly deranged or the man walking by the river
who's kidnapped his child, you saw him,
some daily minacity hovering nearby like a
friendship or an unpaid bill, for this man,
a series of messages, I mean, complete
with essential toiletries and other products,
something in the wind you might say,
just now arriving, the man, or one of us,
or the stranger scuffing up maple leaves,
holding something too close to the vest,
what is called a lack of openness
a feature of the fear-ridden life,
a state of being in which material essential to the production
never gets delivered, and we stand around bewildered on the set,
the outback location with its strings of Chinese lamps
and the tunes playing on a windup device,
where last night we drank
until late and the dreams we referred to seemed not dreams but our lives.

TRUE ART

So I am outside all day some days,
in New York
or on the Rio Grande, and even my posture
is copied
and the inestimable love I attempt
to describe
where there was something Dantesque in her face
that almost killed me, but didn't,
and when she
left, left me unable to respond to circumstance or design,
this, too, like so much else I've quoted
from a stronger source
than my own experience,
lifted, artful sometimes,
sometimes
only a scene at the whole foods store
where a woman in coveralls
berates her ashen-faced desperate child.

TOWNS ALONG THE RIVER

Day frightened me,
daylight did sometimes, the way it vaulted

precisely into place among the dogwoods. You get so
you can't tell anyone what's going on

so you store it in a special chamber
and think about bungalows,

tool sheds and dusty ransacked houses overlooking the
river. *Just address them one by one*—that's what

Father said. And the days
took on number, and coloration, and malediction,

some small derelictous manner in the way we spoke
to strangers, the way the fire truck sat outside the station for months

untended, rusting in the rain. And the farmers
lost everything that year, sure,

while we listened to the new music on the radio
and Mother grew dependent on her medicine.

Time will tell, the principal said
and crossed her heart with the left panel

of her robe, spilling flowers down the front of her,
looking at me as if I might, if I was quick, get what was going on.

DUSK AT HOMER'S

The sun withdraws into its twilight years,
into forgetfulness & dreams.
Hard to forget what once we had,
but I'd rather,

rather move on. Ducks in the city,
wildlife in the city, birds:
a list of sightings
tacked to the St. Luke's garden shed: vireos,

a brown thrasher, tanager, shrike.
Who saw those birds?
Some historian, I guess,
someone with time to kill.

Or now we just say things.
I say she loves me & that's what it is,
say Pesco's still alive,
still talking Aquinas as he cooks.

And that fall when a storm
blew all the leaves out of the trees
and the football field on Saturday was ankle deep
in yellow & red tatters,

we scampered in our satin suits
through them.
An old man in the window is reading a book out loud,
maybe, like me,

skipping the bad parts.
A woman nearby's

got a squared-off look. She took
the average of herself and went with that.

I try to remember what
we used to say about things,
how we put it to ourselves.
I don't know, do you?

I've got time on my hands,
it won't wash off.

DAY 7/24

Each day arrives in pieces, it's easy to put together, every-
one does it, the functions appear, those paid to revolve rapidly begin,
others gape, some welcome despair, a righteousness flaps like tattered flags,
no one believes this crap, each would like to speak truly, live
with no cause for regret,
I take off my fake silver wings and
stare out at the lawn where nothing much is happening, only night
collecting and disposing of itself, the vegetable kingdom, distant uneasy dogs.

COMMON KNOWLEDGE

I'm crossing Sixth again in my dream
carrying *Jules Verne* and the diaries of Chateaubriand,
a small anthology of post-Elizabethan poetry into the park
it's dangerously beautiful today, semitropical in NYC,
sea breezes in the maples and oaks, an Homeric wind
born to blow us off course and out of the flower beds
comes running a black man chased by two white men
and another black, running like you never see anyone
in the city run, disencumbered and fleet, corners,
and gets away, it's wonderful to get away from everything
for once, a property known to each living thing,
I waked thinking of my worries, they're intact, unchanged,
wrote a little, counted on something helping me
it's a solemnly beautiful dawn today in this dream
the malabar daisies and spindrift pink spidery flowers nearby
haven't asked for an explanation and the reversal of fortune
goes unnoticed by some, I'm sure
I realize now there are things I won't get over
ill tides in myself I won't rise above
still I am walking and sometimes wonderment fills me
sometimes despair, thoughts of a gun in a blue drawer
you can't say it's neurotic or even bitter really
and the brisk luxuriance of the late-summer trees,
Mother's funeral where the preacher
got sick in the heat and Buddy said, "She's still laying them out,"
nothing's really enough to reverse the situation, it's clear
about this, a panel of judges
might differ, but then you go outside
in a dream the crippling effects of being alive start up again
the light buffing the rim of your soul, too,
my friend says he's been dreaming all his life

slowly awakening, just now
in the subway on a journey across time
puts his hand out for a boy
to catch him before a plunge into the dark, and feels fine.

RAIN WEST OF MARFA

... the way she put it—what she got from me—
offensive?—not exactly—
dismaying?—
the way I enclosed her
the word she used—
her inside me—I thought
of my years in West Texas—
       the leaves of the bur oak
turning the deep red of kings—

... just yesterday someone
asked about her
said something about plurality being imperfect
apprehension of reality

in her eyes a penetrating greed
avidity
staring at each other's bodies

she was older than me

          * * *

we'd talk about how far we'd come

hard rain in the P.M.
streets awash
and the alley a riverway
for leaves and bugs

we used to wade the Rio Grande
      get a cold one

at the casita
about sunset wade back

—an irrepressible tilt to her perception

one crisis after another

she said, I think something is wrong with me

* * *

loved hotels

passionate, a critic said about the book
she wrote
speaking of us
but I never saw it that way
—until then—

the harsh, repressive
        lovemaking
        dense,
a nervous, complex
                distancing
never dissuaded
or forgot
        —yet both emerged
                at orgasm

a path through the chaparral

* * *

we never even talked about children

never owned anything

each first moment the last best

I'd walk around saying
        I don't love her
        I have to leave

went home to Texas
        she rode away on a pony
                gone for hours
said she'd crossed
                into Mexico, met
new friends
        read out loud
                cooked,
discovered gold, swam naked
                in a tank—her hair matted

a calm to her
        compact surety
a simplicity of manner
                that didn't last

we were both unfaithful
        mine worse
reconciled
        she said, "We must not part"

                * * *

the slim-hipped country bees
working the road daisies
after a rain
like a school of tiny yellow fishes
congregation
not "envelopment"
a gathering, this—

          * * *

supra-imposed, the slant
    —a carelessness
        unsound
she rarely cried
      after talks w/ her mother
        she'd be mean
        for days

her thick hair like a mysterious country
     closed for years
        strange untrellised
a stillness, silence
     her hair like a usefulness
       superseded
     by immaculation
        a densely worded
          expression
complex
    I loved it best disheveled

          * * *

She said, "This world is hell,"
    thought bulging

broke off in midsentence
    w/ a clicking sound
    gurgling sound
    strangling
        on ideas

we had a clear picture of life

trust
complicity
    —absolute fidelity
        like black-eyed Susans
        grease
        immortality

you never mistake it

NEW JERSEY TRANSIT

Rusted up industrial natures you spy
across the river, warehouses with roofs smashed in and
dunked docks, old boats forsaking travel now.
Am I far from home? someone asks,
as someone does every day. A life hammered, collapsed together,
spade work, the soul gone limp
from loving people you never liked. Spring turning the woods pale
with fright. A ballplayer picks up his baby girl
and they both laugh, but you are calculating
how long it takes to put something like this together.
Plumbers, young divorced women
returning to their relatives on the New Jersey Transit,
a college out the window, young people
don't know much yet, they're not tired out,
haven't learned the price for these latest thoughts,
the going rate for love, and the one where
you spread vast wings and collect the children under them.

THE MOMENT PRECEDING

A reverie, small fabrication
of silence, some amulet or woven purse,
some moment in which the languor
is preceded by quiet, this moment comes
first in the dawnlight,
a deep and peculiar clarity, peered into,
some color scheme barely perceptible, this
silence
in which the rigorously fought-out nightwar, the peace
established through centuries of tedious
negotiation, is not blown away
or thrown aside but breached nonetheless
by a simple, barely detectable epistemology,
this tiny shift in conciousness itself,
expressed just now by the scent of gardenias.

LITTLE PARADISE

Beside the train tracks, in gullies
where old men got down on their knees because they were told to,
it gets perfect for a second,
      starlight lines up with the earth,
the black ripple of the hillside—
nothing to us now, or anything at all—
perfected by the nod of attention, the space
passing between one thing seen and another
as you lean toward it—
      the day, that's failed at everything else,
bringing this up—the momentum
carrying the light toward you,
the little stream and its backup bushes,
the familiar way the bugs
transfer their desires to the soft summer air,
      all this part of the paradisiacal improbability
of the mix, the texture of plant life,
the day grinding figuratively to a halt
or coming smoothly forth, the
little animals prepared for whatever's next,
a design maybe, or some
particular fitting accomplished,
      no one knows exactly, and the cracked
purple rocks that look like painted bones,
and the bugs, which stop everything they're doing
and then start up again, as if that's how it goes.

OLD NOBODIES TRAVELING ALONE

Like the hand of God

sweeping backward along a passing train,
like a hand
moving down hip-length hair,

say coppery hair, summer in Antwerp,

lindens in bloom
and the architectural students
giving up righteousness for drugs,

around then
when reports burned
under shady circumstances,

then—like the hand of God we said—

all these elements, corsages
floating in the bowl
you dunked your face in,

love all razory
and dulcé—the time before

you conformed
to the unfathomable circumstances
of your next position—

just then, the robin said,
before I could really sing,

. . .

we were speaking of turncoats,
tableaux,
the formal arrangement

in which the circumstantial lover

alternated with his own dismay,
the two of them—we're part of this—
contingent, fretful, moving steadily

across the space that was left.

THE WILDERNESS

I think of cities that have vanished into time.
I'm sister to the rain. The trees plunge like dolphins
and the city's a ship diving in the sea.
Everything vanished just a moment ago.
I recall my shame at having to watch my father
be humiliated. They made him recant everything he'd said.
And then praise them. My father the poet, who was never strong.

Even in a city, my friend says,
all you have to do is look up to see wilderness. He means the sky,
weather and such. Once he lived in a hogan out in Arizona.
And got caught sexually pestering an Indian schoolgirl and
went to jail for it. Then he moved to New York
and became a fabric designer. He has a shop over on Madison.

Carthage. Ninevah. Chandrapore.
Mostly the important cities didn't disappear.

"We took a boat up the Ganges, but we had to get out;
all the floating corpses made my wife sick. You can
get too much of that in a hurry. We caught a train
and that was much better, though even in the first-class car
we couldn't avoid the smells. India is in the smells,
don't let anyone tell you different."

AND MY SISTERS
ARE NOT WITHOUT THEIR REASONS —for selling out that is.

As a child I thought I'd like to live
on the Côte d'Azur,
which I imagined to be blue-lit, pale and empty,
bare white rocks
and palm trees under a ferocious uncolored sun.
I thought Robinson Crusoe
lived on the Côte d'Azur with his faithful Friday.

And Mother sang in the bath—suicide songs,
Father called them.

                   * * *

We drank Sanka out on the screened porch
and listened to the owls calling from the empty lot next door.
Grandfather wanted Uncle Peedee to build on that lot,
but he wouldn't. He bought a house down the street
and lived there with his wife, Maude the Electrified Woman.
She was old, Maude, she had hair the color of smoke and twitched.

I am divided against myself, mean sometimes,
but I have decided *I am not a mean person.* My wife
was mean—I said that to the judge. Oh sure, he said
and snickered. My father's last years
were spent quietly, reading Proust. He'd glance up
from time to time—a look of torment in his face.
You'd wait for that, for the sad, ugly expression
of regret tinged with shame and fury, and we grew
to hate it. We wrote about it in our diaries.
Three sisters and a brother locked into our rooms
scribbling.

* * *

Dear Diary : Today I caught a dose of father's "Look"
and wanted to kill him. Am I crazy?

The Monkey Woman—that's what my sisters
called my wife. They could be cruel, my sisters,
but they had no power. "We live in South Georgia,"
Arlene wrote, "at one with the bugs and the snakes."
Now they never leave the house.

I was small for my age. They say you never get
over something like that, but I think I have.
As an adult I'm a little short,
but not too much. If I was a midget I think it
would be worse. "You get a woman to love you,"
my uncle said, "you'll be okay." His squinty wife
Maude peered down at me from her
electrified distance, head crackling with static.

My grandmother could picture anyone naked.

* * *

And sometimes I think the sunset
hates the darkening houses.

When the robbers made Father take his clothes off
and kneel before them I wished I could have fainted.
I see the vanes of my mother's tragic face
behind the rain, all that,
which I have explained to you in my letter
and would like to spend an evening talking about, if you'd let me.
Please respond to this note posthaste.

_____

DUSK, LIKE THE MESSIAH

for Michael Block

Dusk, like the Messiah, appears everywhere all at once while we are thinking
how love never really lets up and everyone,
so we've come to realize, is innocent of his crimes,
just as they told us—the little talkers and
spokesmen out in the daylight, the ravers and constant jokers who
never get anywhere (they mentioned this)—and once again a surprising
and unencumbered tenderness seeps into crevices and conversations where
    the one speaking,
for just a second, looks up from the discourse and goes quiet as if he gets it.

Made in the USA
Las Vegas, NV
20 February 2023

67875286R00059